IN THIS TOPZ ...

Hello!!!

I have recently started wearing glasses, and was described by a friend as looking like a wise old owl! It made me think that if all it took to become wise was to put on a pair of glasses – then everyone should wear them! We would all probably like to be wise ... and I don't think you necessarily have to be really old before you can be wise. Being wise involves knowledge, experience and good judgment, and is also about becoming aware of or informed about something. Each year we can all grow a little bit wiser, and I hope this issue of *Topz* will help you, especially where we look at what the Bible says about wisdom in the book of James.

We can be wise in the way we look after God's world, how we choose to have fun, how we treat other people and how we spend our time and money. So I hope and pray that the Topz Gang will have helped you to grow a little wiser by the time you reach the end of these notes. If you think God has helped you to be wise in any situation, please do write and tell me. I always love to hear how you're all doing ☺

See you again in the next issue, when we'll all be just a little bit older – and hopefully wiser!

Lyrette

P.S. Hope you like our new-look TOPZ!?

The Bible books

HOW TO USE Topz

It may be that some of you haven't looked inside a Bible very much before. If so, here's a few helpful hints:

1 Each day *Topz* has a Bible reading. It's shown like this:

Genesis 25 v 2-5

2

To find this, turn to the Contents page near the front of your Bible and look for the name of the **book** – which in the example is Genesis. Now find the **page** this book starts on and turn to it.

3 You will have to turn on a few pages now to get to the right chapter.

4 Now look for the verse numbers which will be in smaller type. The chapter and verse will look like this:

Chapter   Verse

5 After reading the Bible passage, go back to the *Topz* page and see what it says. Each day ends with a prayer and sometimes an action point too.

To solve the puzzles in *Topz* you will need a **Good News Bible**.

If you don't want to turn to the Contents page of your Bible all the time, you will see we've listed all the Bible books in order for you (see left). The ones you'll be reading from in this *Topz* are highlighted with a star ✦.

Use this *Topz* Marker to keep your place in *Topz*.
Cut it out and stick it to a piece of card to strengthen it.

A SPECIAL CITY

Topz pictures of famous cities.

By John.
Rome – city of
seven hills.

By Sarah.
London – Tower Bridge
and Big Ben.

What's
your picture,
Benny?

That's Jerusalem
of course!
The 'holey' city!

Benny was making a joke. The word
'holy' (spelt right!) really means
**'special to God'. Our Bible
readings will tell us how and why
this city was special to God ...**

3

What's in a name?

Did you know ...
that most names of people and places mean something?

JOHN is from a word meaning 'God is gracious'

DAVE means 'beloved'

SARAH means 'the princess'

JESUS means 'Saviour'

The old city of Jerusalem was first of all called 'Salem', which means 'peace'. Melchizedek, the king of Salem, was therefore the 'King of Peace'. He reminds us of Jesus, who is called 'The Prince of Peace'.

Think of your home. Think of a really good name for it. Draw a picture and write the new name by it. Maybe you coul< send it in to Topz?

PRAY

Dear Lord Jesus, please teach me how to let You be King of my life. Amen.

ACTION

Wherever Jesus rules, He brings His peace.

City of David

David was the first of Israel's kings to live in Jerusalem. He made it his capital city.

Jerusalem was a fortress, built on a hill. It was very difficult to capture, but David found a way to drive the Jebusites out. **Which of these was his way in?**

(Answer on page)

PRAY

Lord God, nothing can stand in Your way. May Your will be done on earth! Amen.

ACTION

Why did David become a good and strong king (v 10)? You can learn from this!

City of singing

The **Covenant Box** was covered inside and out with gold. The Ten Commandments were kept in it. It was very holy and the tent where the Covenant Box was kept was the special place for meeting to worship God.

This is probably what the Covenant Box looked like.

Jerusalem was a place of singing and dancing in praise of God.

Read the mirror message

By bringing the Covenant Box to Jerusalem the city became a holy place where people came to worship God.

PRAY

Thank You, Lord Jesus, that I can worship You wherever I am. Amen.

ACTION

Why not write out your favourite praise or worship song and illustrate it.

City of the Temple

David did not want God's Covenant Box to stay in a tent!

God told David's son, Solomon, to build a Temple for the box, where the people could worship Him.

Solomon did his best to make the Temple a beautiful place for God to live in.

Fit these columns in their correct places to read a message from 1 Corinthians 3 v 16.

2	3	4	5	6	7	8	9	10	11	12	13	14	15	16	17
r	e	l	y		y	o	u			k	n		w		
a	t		y		u		a			e			o	d	's
m	p	l	e		a	n	d			t	h		t		
d	's		S		i	r	i				l		v	e	s
y	o	u													

7
o
P
!
G
a
i

14
o
G
a
i

2
u
h
e
o
n

11
r
t

Dear Lord Jesus, thank You so much that You have chosen to live with all who trust You. Amen.

ACTION

If you trust Jesus, He comes to live with you. You are His temple! Keep your life beautiful for Him.

City of safety

Another name for Jerusalem is Zion.
The people felt safe inside the city for they believed
it was God's city. Jesus is like a strong city around us,
if we trust Him.

Help!

What might Jo
be thinking of
such a time?

Colour the blocks and draw lines
across from 'x' to 'x' to find a prayer
from Psalm 119 v 117 for John to pray.

PRAY

HOLD ME AND I
WILL BE SAFE

Do you feel
frightened
about
something?
Ask God to
keep you safe

ACTION

God often keeps us safe from
harm when we don't even
realise we are in danger!

City of foolish people

Some Jews thought like this ...

(Read each word backwards.)

esehT sllaw era os
kciht, ew era efas
edisni

dnA melasureJ si
s'doG yloh ytic ...

oS eH t'now tel
gnihtyna dab
neppah ot su.

But what did Jeremiah tell them? Jeremiah 7 v 5

C _ _ _ _ _ _   t _ _
w _ _ y _ _
a _ _ l _ _ _ _ _.

The people were doing a lot of very bad things, so God said He could no longer keep them safe.

PRAY

Dear Lord Jesus, thank You for loving me so much. Help me to trust You and obey You. Please keep me safe. Amen.

9

City of sadness

Move each letter forward one place in the alphabet.
a = b, b = c, z = a, etc.

1. What had the people become? (v 3)

r k z u d r

....

2. Who goes to the Temple now? (v 4)

mn nmd

....

3. Look in verse 5 and write down why Jerusalem had been destroyed by her enemies.

....
....
....
....
....
....

How sad! And all because th people would not obey God.

PRAY Dear Lord Jesus, thank You that when I have asked You to forgive my sin, I don't have to be sad any more. Amen.

ACTION Is there something in your life that makes God sad? Ask Him to help you change.

City of joy

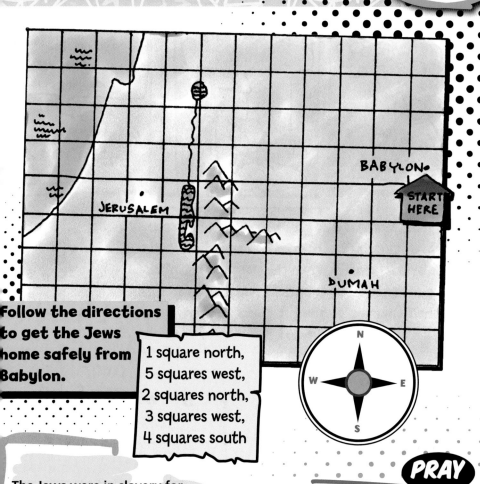

Follow the directions to get the Jews home safely from Babylon.

1 square north,
5 squares west,
2 squares north,
3 squares west,
4 squares south

The Jews were in slavery for 70 years while Jerusalem lay in ruins. Now God was about to bring them home again. God had not forgotten His people, He was going to forgive them and bring them home where they would be happy again.

PRAY

I am glad, Lord Jesus, that You never forget me or leave me on my own. Amen.

ACTION

Have a think about what your home means to you.

11

City of trouble

Tell me what's wrong.

It's school. I can't do the sums. And everyone's laughing at me!

Are you having a problem with some work you can't do, or is something else bothering you? When the people went back to Jerusalem they had problems. The city was in ruins and their enemies laughed at them. Look in verse 9. **What did the people do?**

Follow the lines to find Nehemiah's message to the people (v 20). Start here

o r o w l f g s

u

o r

t f

u G d i l i h

PRAY

Dear Lord Jesus, thank You that You help me, and thank You for people like parents and teachers who help me too. Amen.

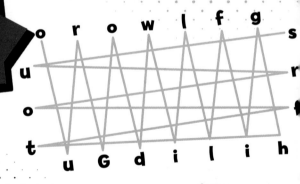

ACTION

In verse 9, the people prayed and also did all they could themselves. When you have a problem, remember to pray and ask God how He can help you solve it.

City of the King

Make your way through the streets of Jerusalem and read a message to the people from Psalm 149 v 2.

START HERE

Many Jewish kings had been crowned in Jerusalem. Now Jesus is coming as King of all, to give His life for all people.

Never had Jerusalem welcomed a greater king within her walls.

PRAY

Lord Jesus, I worship You and praise You, for You are the great King. Amen.

ACTION

Think of three reasons why you can praise King Jesus:

....

....

....

....

....

....

City of the future

One day God will make a new Jerusalem.

Fill in the missing words using the words in the word-bank.

WORD-BANK

glory moon
sinful love
city Jesus

The heavenly _____ has no temple, for God Himself is there. His _____ shines there, so neither sun nor _____ is needed. No bad or _____ thing is there, and only those who _____ and trust in _____ will enter the city.

It'll be great to be there!

PRAY

Dear God,
I'm looking forward to that great day and Your brilliant place. Amen.

ACTION

Read Revelation 21 v 2-4 to see how happy we will be in this city, because of what God will do.

14

TOPZ GOES GREEN

Topz may be too young to vote, but they are not too young to take notice of the world around them. Many political parties and, more importantly, God, want us to take better care of the world in which we live. **Read on and you may get some ideas about what you can do to keep our world 'green'.**

The earth is the Lord's

This is my tree!

No it's not! It's in my garden.

Yes, but all the branches are in my garden.

From world governments, right down to small children, people fight over land and things which they claim are theirs, but –

Read the words in the readaround to see what the Bible says (from Deuteronomy 10 v 14).

To the Lord b
h e a v e n s ; t h
t l s o , a n d e e
s a o n i t . v l
e g n i h t y r e o
h s i h s i h t r a
g i h e h t n e v e

PRAY

Dear Lord Jesus, help me not to be selfish with the things You have given me. Amen.

ACTION

Nothing we have is our own. God has simply let us have the use of the things in His world.

Full of what?

Put the squares in their correct places.

9 104 v 13	**5** with	**2** earth
4 filled	**1** The	**7** blessings
8 Psalm	**6** Your	**3** is

1	**2**	**3**
4	**5**	**6**
7	**8**	**9**

What beautiful things has God placed around you for your enjoyment, to smell, see, hear, feel and taste?

_____
_____
_____
_____

PRAY

Thank You, Lord Jesus, for giving me my senses (like sight and hearing) to enjoy this world. Amen.

ACTION

If you know the song, 'All things bright and beautiful', why not write down a verse and the chorus, and then illustrate it with some of your favourite plants, animals etc. We'd love to see it if you want to send it to Topz!

Park-keepers

When God made the world, He did not put up signs saying:

But in order to look after our world, signs are often needed to tell us what to do, and suggest ways we can keep it looking beautiful.

Read the code to see what God did say.
(Move each letter one letter forward: z = a, a = b etc.)

Dminx lx vnqkc.

_ _ _ _ _ _ — _ _ _ _ _ .

Knnj zesdq hs.

_ _ _ _ _ _ _ _ _ — _ _ .

PRAY

Heavenly Father, help me to do my bit to keep the world the way You want it. Amen.

When you see signs like those above, obey them, because most are there for a good reason.

The sea and everything in it

Many seals and other creatures have died or been harmed because of chemicals that factories have poured into the rivers which flow into the sea.

Beaches are spoiled and fish and birds killed by oil slicks.

Remember what God has said ...

1. I am putting
2. you in charge
3. of the
4. fish, the birds
5. and all
6. the wild
7. animals

PRAY

Thank You, Lord Jesus, for the many kinds of animals and creatures You have made. Amen.

ACTION

Care for animals, and if you have pets, look after them properly.

19

Smoke + rain = acid rain

Smoke damages your health. How many kinds of smoking are in the picture?

(Answer on page 73)

Smoke takes harmful chemicals up into the air which mix with the rain and come down again in some places in the world. This 'acid rain' is bad for trees and plants. It may not be a problem where you live, but we must all help to stop it by making less smoke.

PRAY

Lord, help me to see what I can do to improve Your world. Amen.

ACTION

Think of a title for today's Bible verses and write it here.

_____

_____

Take a deep breath

By cutting down and burning forests we are destroying trees which give us the oxygen we need to breathe.

What kinds of trees are these?

2nd word

1st word

Boo Hoo

1. _ _ _ _ _ _ _ _   _ _ _ _ _ _

2. _ _ _ _ _ _ _ _ _

3. _ _ _   _ _ _ _

4. _ _ _ _ _   _ _ _ _

(Answer on page 73)

Treat trees and plants with respect – don't harm them ... your very breath depends on them.

PRAY

Thank You, Lord Jesus, for the beauty of plants and trees and for the clean air they give to me. Amen.

ACTION

If you get the chance, join in a tree-planting campaign, or plant some flowers.

21

Who made this mess?

God's gift to you.

God made the earth and it was good! What do you think made God so pleased with His creation?

(Answers on page 73)

1. It was full of God's goodness.
   ☐ YES ☐ NO

2. The beaches were dirty and oily.
   ☐ YES ☐ NO

3. Everything was full of life – growing, producing fruit and new life.
   ☐ YES ☐ NO

4. The rivers were full of pollution (chemicals).
   ☐ YES ☐ NO

People have spoiled the earth. How do you think God feels about it?

PRAY

Lord Jesus, I am sorry people have spoiled Your world. Please forgive us. Amen.

ACTION

Do you take care of your part of the world – your pets, toys, bedroom, garden?

Who's to blame?

ome people are cutting down orests to make room for cattle so hat people can eat more meat.

Factory owners sometimes pollute rivers with waste material because this is cheaper than getting rid of waste in other ways.

Today's reading gives two reasons why people mess up our world.
(Fill in the blank spaces)

1. They are g _ _ _ _ _
   for money (v 22)

2. They are l _ _ _ (v 24)

Can't you throw your rubbish in the bin?

PRAY

Dear Lord Jesus, please forgive me when I am greedy or lazy. Amen.

ACTION

Look at the pictures on this page. Who is being greedy? Who is being lazy?

23

Rulers or ruiners?

Across

1. Man is in charge of the birds and the _____. (v 8)
3. God's greatness is seen ___ all the world. (v 1)
5. God set the moon and the _____ in their places. (v 3)
7. God made man _____ over everything. (v 6)
9. God made the ____. (v 3)

Down

2. Where does God's praise reach? (v 1)
4. Is God happy when man messes up the world?
6. The Lord is ____ Lord. (v 1)
8. God's praise reaches ___ to the heavens. (v 1)

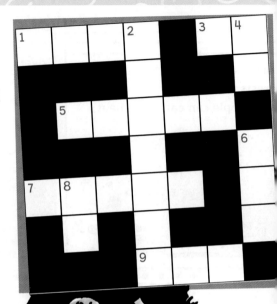

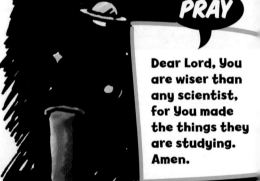

PRAY

Dear Lord, You are wiser than any scientist, for You made the things they are studying. Amen.

ACTION

Let's try not to ruin the world over which God made us rulers. For example, only buy 'ozone-friendly' sprays (ozone in the sky protects us from the harmful rays of the sun).

THE GANG'S GREEN TIPS

People are getting more serious about caring for the environment – so the Gang are seeing where they can learn and take action. Here are some hints and tips from the Gang about how they are trying to be 'green'!

'I will almost always walk when I need to get somewhere. Sometimes I ride my bike if it's too far to walk. I try to get my friends to do the same. I, along with the rest of my family, also recycle everything from glass bottles to drinks cans.'

'I never used to switch off the lights when I left a room, but I heard how I can save resources and energy by turning them off when they don't need to be on and now I always try to remember to do that when I leave.'

'Our school has been doing an eco-schools project. We have been designing and building our gardens and going out to plant wild flower seeds so there are more flowers for birds and insects. We are also putting up posters saying, "Don't drop litter, put it in the bin". We have set up an eco-schools club after school to learn more about the environment too.'

'I asked my teacher if we could do something to help and now there are two huge paper recycling bins in each classroom at school.'

'I try to get pencils and stationery made from recycled paper cups and newspapers.'

'I am making sure I don't drop litter on the floor, and if I see someone I know doing it I politely ask them not to.'

get my mum to take her own bag to the shops rather than using plastic bags. I think everybody needs to do much more to save the environment though ... the anet won't save itself you know!'

You can find out more at the Young People's Trust for the Environment @ **www.ypte.org.uk**

Why not design a poster campaigning for people to care about the environment generally, or about a specific area that you care a lot about, and send it to us at *Topz*.

DODGEMS & DIPPERS

IT'S A LOVELY SUNNY DAY, SO TOPZ HAVE PERSUADED DANNY'S DAD TO DRIVE THEM TO THE SEASIDE.

Come on, let's go to the fair!

I love these rides.

Shall I look after your candyfloss for you, Dave?

Not likely!

Maybe I should have listened to you, Danny!

Good advice is hard to get, so it's wise to listen to others instead of being stubborn, thinking that you are always right. That is what it means to be arrogant.

PRAY

Lord, when I am given good advice give me the good sense to take it. Amen.

DODGEMS AND DIPPERS

Arguments or fights are not the way to settle differences. Rather, be fair, loving and generous while always sticking up for what is right.

PRAY

Lord, help me to get along with other people without arguing or fighting. Amen.

27

DODGEMS AND DIPPERS

This is the last of my money.

Let's put our money together for one last ride.

Come in number 6.

He can't mean us, we're number 9.

HAHA

It's good that Topz could laugh when things went wrong – though perhaps it would have been more sensible if they hadn't overloaded the boat! Try to keep on smiling, even when things are difficult. Being grumpy or short-tempered certainly won't improve anything.

PRAY

Lord, please help me to look on the bright side and be a cheerful person. Amen.

DODGEMS AND DIPPERS

During summertime there are often teams of people holding what are called 'holiday missions' or clubs at the seaside or in parks. Watch out for them this summer. Say hello to them.

PRAY

Pray for people helping at holiday clubs, that God will use them to encourage children to put their trust in Jesus.

DODGEMS AND DIPPERS

This is a race to set up a deck chair and sit in it.

That looks easy!

Finished!

And me.

You have to hand it to Benny, he really sticks at it!

It's great to be able to say that you don't give up easily. When God begins something, He finishes it too! He's making us more like Jesus by helping us to change our behaviour, and He's not going to give up on us.

PRAY

Dear Lord Jesus, please help me to stick at following You every day. Amen.

DODGEMS AND DIPPERS

I want you to use shells, rocks and anything else you can find to make a Bible verse in the sand.

This is a good one.

I think you've made a slight mistake!

The kettle on thousands of hills

Read Psalm 50 v 10 to discover Topz' mistake. We all make mistakes or get things wrong at times – that's part of learning – but never be afraid to ask someone when you need an explanation. A disciple is someone who is still learning.

PRAY

Dear Lord Jesus, thank You for my teachers, friends and family who help me to understand how to follow You. Amen.

31

KNIGHTS OF THE WAY

IN DAYS OF OLD WHEN KNIGHTS WERE BOLD ...

Dreams and real life are often far apart. But the Christian life is an exciting journey. **Arise, Sir Knight of the Glorious Way, and serve your King!**

Good knight

Be followers of that which is good.

Look at verses 14 and 15 and draw a line to match up these ways of doing good:

Encourage

    everyone

Help

    the timid (nervous)

Be patient with

    all people

Do good to

    the weak

How much 'good' can the Good Knight find in this puzzle?

Use the letters of this puzzle to spell the word 'good' three times. You can use the letters twice, but the joining lines only once.

(Answer on page 73)

START HERE

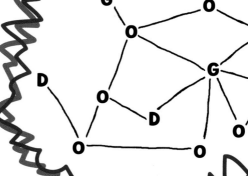

PRAY

Ask for God's help to do good things with your life.

ACTION

Write here one person you can be good to this week:

_____

_____

33

Throwing down the gauntlet

A knight would sometimes challenge another knight to a duel or fight by throwing down his gauntlet (large metal glove).

Jesus called people like Simon, Andrew, James and John to serve in His kingdom. It would be a challenge, but Jesus knew the battles they would face.

Find six differences between the two pictures.

Ouch!

Ouch!

PRAY

Lord Jesus, I face battles too, sometimes. Please make me strong in those times. Amen.

Trust King Jesus to help you in the difficulties and challenges you face.

34

Knights of the round table

Find five things which don't belong in this picture.

(Answer on page 73)

Knights helped each other. They stuck up for each other and were bound together by an oath or promise. Jesus' friends should be like that too!

That is why we need to ...

(Put the first letter of each picture beneath it.)

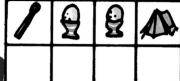

PRAY

Lord Jesus, I belong to You and with other Christians. Help me to love and appreciate them. Amen.

ACTION

Where do you meet with others to learn about following Jesus? Why is it important to meet together?

35

Topz Things to Do
BITZ

If you're on holiday from school over the next few weeks here are a couple of things to keep you busy and having fun ...

Paul's Photo Frame

If you have a favourite holiday photo you could make this frame to keep it in. You'll need:

- A piece of stiff card
- Several flat pieces of Lego
- Glue
- Photo

– Cut a square or rectangle of card approximately 3cm larger all the way round than the photo you want to frame
– Stick the photo in the middle of the card
– Building outwards from the photo, stick on the flat pieces of Lego in your own design
– Build a base for the frame to stand on.

Sarah's Pink Lemonade

This is Sarah's favourite cold drink. To make some for you and your friends you'll need:

- 8 lemons, plus extra slices to serve
- 200g caster sugar, plus extra to taste
- 140g raspberries, plus extra to serve
- ice, to serve

– Grate the zest from the lemons with a peeler or grater, removing as little white pith as possible
– Juice the lemons and mix the juice, zest, sugar and raspberries with 1.2 litres of boiling water
– Let it cool, then sieve, pressing juice through with the back of a spoon
– Pour into jugs, add sugar to taste and chill
– To serve, add a few lemon slices, raspberries and lots of ice.

Army of knights

What an army of knights this king has!

And what an army God has! Find their names in verse 32.

G _ _ _ _ _ _   B _ _ _ _ _   S _ _ _ _ _ _   J _ _ _ _ _ _ _ _   D _ _ _ _

(Answers on page 72)

S _ _ _ _ _ _   P _ _ _ _ _ _ _ _

To look at them, you might not think that all the knights of God's army were mighty men. Verse 34 says: 'They were weak, but became strong.'

To see how, fill in the dotted shapes and check with verse 39.

ACTION

When you feel weak, remember you are starting exactly where great men and women began.

Use your sword!

The Good Knight's sword was used to fight evil – and so is the Bible, the Word of God.

Find five words written on the shield which appear in Hebrews 4 v 12, and describe the Word of God.

```
A C T I V E T
L U A E S C A
I T L B D O L
V S H A R P B
E J U D G E S
```

It is A _ _ _ _,
A _ _ _ _ _,
S _ _ _ _.
It C _ _ _ and
J _ _ _ _ _.

Because the Bible is 'sharp', it points out what is good and what is bad in our lives.

PRAY

Lord God, thank You that the Bible is powerful and alive. I pray that it will help me to understand what You want for my life. Amen.

ACTION

If God speaks to you through reading the Bible, make sure you listen, and act on what He says. You might like to write and tell us about it.

In days of old

The people of Israel often looked back to the time when God parted the Red Sea so they could walk through and escape the army of Egypt. Josie was looking back ...

Read backwards: day. each us for done has He things of think also should we But past. the in done has God what see and back look to thing wonderful a is It

START HERE

PRAY

Lord Jesus, thank You for what You have done for me in the past and every day. Amen.

ACTION

Write here one thing God has done for you in the past week:

_____

_____

Damsel in distress

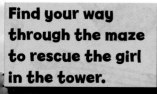

Find your way through the maze to rescue the girl in the tower.

Use a mirror to read the message reflected in the moat.

care for everyone

God wants us to show thoughtfulness for those who are upset, hurt or in distress.

You don't have to be a knight to help them!

PRAY

Lord, I want You to use my lips, my hands and my feet to help those who are hurt or in trouble. Amen.

ACTION

Can you think of someone who might need or be grateful for your help this week?

41

Attack and defence

Draw a circle around each item which a knight could use to defend himself.

When King David was sad or had a problem, he was glad he could turn to God. He felt like a soldier under attack who could run inside a fort and be safe there.

PRAY

Heavenly Father,
I'm glad to know I am safe because I am protected by Your love and care. Thank You. Amen.

ACTION

Proverbs 18 v 10 is a great verse which describes how we can be safe. Read it and see if you can memorise it.

Shields on

Knights' shields showed who they served. Copy the shield designs onto the shield of the knight who owns them:

As a soldier of Jesus, imagine you have a shield and shield design. On some paper draw your own shield design 'To show who you serve'.

Send your shield design to Topz and we will print the best in a future issue.

SIR WILLIAM OF THE THREE KEYS

RICHARD THE LION-HEART

SIR EDWARD OF SHERWOOD FOREST

PRAY

Lord Jesus, I am proud to serve You. Amen.

SIR GEORGE OF IRONGATE

SIR JOHN OF LOXLEY CASTLE

ACTION

People can see who you belong to by the way you live.

Joust in time

Sometimes knights had competitions with lances. This was called jousting. They did it to win fame and respect – or even to win the king's daughter in marriage.

Take a pen or pencil as your lance. With your eyes shut, you have just one go to hit this knight before he hits you! Prod the page and see who wins!

THUNDER

THUNDER

THUND

Have an aim in life - don't just follow the crowd. Instead, live for Jesus each day. Make it your aim to please Him in all the things you do.

PRA

Lord, help me to know that pleasing You is the path to happiness. Amen.

ACTION

God will say a great big 'WELL DONE' to all who have done their best to live for Him.

Bold Sir Benny of Holly Hill

Here's Benny dressed up as a Knight of the Way! Have fun colouring him in!

GET WISE

Over the next few days we're going to be reading from the book of James ...

Mrs Oglethorpe is awful. As soon as I can do my sums – she gives me harder sums!

But if she doesn't give you harder sums – how will you get any better?

Today's reading teaches us that God lets us go through difficulties to help us learn how to keep on trusting Him. Wisdom means tackling problems God's way. **If we get stuck, what must we do?**

6 **the**	4 **gives**	3 **who**
9 **need**	1 **Ask**	8 **we**
2 **God**	5 **all**	7 **wisdom**

Put the squares in order to find out.

1	2	3
4	5	6
7	8	9

PRAY Are you facing a problem? Ask God for the wisdom you need to get through it.

Here today, gone tomorrow

CHRISTINE IS A NEW GIRL IN JOSIE'S CLASS. ONE DAY JOSIE INVITED HER TO SUNDAY SCHOOL.

Would you like to come with me on Sundays?

We used to go to church, but now we've got a big boat and we spend Sundays on it.

It's not wrong to have lots of money – but it's not good if it makes you forget God. If a rich person relies too much on money for happiness, God is not pleased. **Why? Match the jigsaw pieces.**

rely on

on money

her to

him or

God, not

God wants

to teach

PRAY Dear Lord Jesus, money comes and goes, but You are always the same. I am so glad I can trust You. Amen.

ACTION

Don't forget – money isn't bad. It does a lot of good. But true happiness can only come through knowing God, and cannot be bought.

47

Clear out the rubbish

John can't close his cupboard door because it's so untidy and full of rubbish.

What should he do?

....

....

....

It won't go in!

START HERE

God —— things.
good
of —— wants
full
life —— your
be
to

Jesus came to save us from bad habits and sin – the rubbish that fills our lives.

PRAY

Dear Lord Jesus, please help me to change and get rid of the 'rubbish' in my life. Amen.

ACTION

God can only fill your life with good things when you are willing to empty out the rubbish.

Mirror, mirror on the wall

As soon as he walked away from the mirror, Dave forgot all about combing his hair! When your Bible tells you to do something, put it into action – don't forget!

Try copying the mirror image of Sarah.

PRAY

Thank You, Lord Jesus, for the wisdom in the Bible and for the truth I find there about You. Amen.

ACTION

Why should we obey the Bible and do what God says (v 25)?

Take care of them

(Answers on page 73)

What kinds of people we should care for can you find in the wordsearch?

(There are six: some are in today's Bible reading and these pictures.) The words may go up, down, across or diagonally.

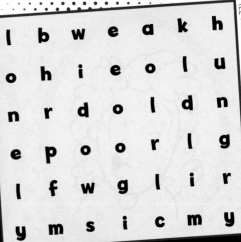

```
l  b  w  e  a  k  h
o  h  i  e  o  l  u
n  r  d  o  l  d  n
e  p  o  o  r  l  g
l  f  w  g  l  i  r
y  m  s  i  c  m  y
```

PRAY

Pray for the poor, hungry and homeless people in your country.

ACTION

Your church notice board may show you ways in which you can help needy people.

Rich man, poor man

All the girls in my class want to be friends with Christine.

It's because she's got a swimming pool.

They don't want to be friends with me because I live in a flat.

It's not wrong to have lots of money (see note on 7th August) but it is wrong to think that living in a big house makes someone better than other people.

PRAY

I praise You, Jesus, that whether I am old or young, rich or poor, I am just as important to You as anyone else. Amen.

Have you met this sort of problem?

Read the code to see what is important to God.

⬤ = e, □ = o, ◆ = u

H□w m◆ch w⬤
□ve G□d

ACTION

Today's verses say that it's wrong to be specially nice to people just because they are rich or important.

51

Dead or alive!

True Christians show their love for others and their faith in God by what they do. **Follow the lines to find what these famous Christians have done.**

Doctor Barnardo William Wilberforce Florence Nightingale William Booth

HELPED FEED AND CLOTHE THE POOR

HELPED TO END SLAVERY

CARED FOR THE SICK

CARED FOR ORPHANS

PRAY

Thank You, Lord Jesus, for those who care for the rich and poor. Amen.

ACTION

Is your faith in God dead or alive? Can you think of something you can do to show your love for someone you know or someone who is in need of help?

Seeing the invisible

We can't see the wind, so how do we know it is there?

Electricity cannot be seen, so how do we know it is there?

So how can we see a Christian's faith?

We know about wind and electricity because of the things they do. A Christian's faith has to be shown by what he or she does - we must try to bring God's love into people's lives.

PRAY

Dear Lord Jesus, help me to truly depend on You, to trust You and show Your love in all I do. Amen.

ACTION

Think back over the past week. Have there been times when you've been able to show your faith?

Under control

How much control do you have?

Hold a small mirror along the dotted line and, looking ONLY in the mirror, follow the path from 'x' to 'x' without going off it onto the grass.

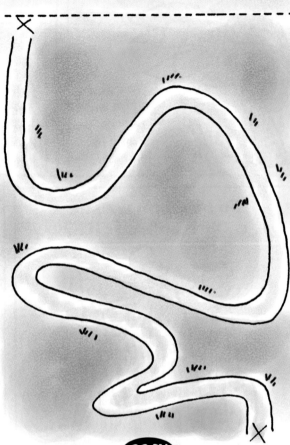

How much control do you have over your tongue? Do you say things for which you are sorry later? Our words can either hurt other people or help them.

PRAY

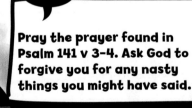

Pray the prayer found in Psalm 141 v 3-4. Ask God to forgive you for any nasty things you might have said.

ACTION

The more you use your tongue for saying good things the better you'll feel, and you'll get on better with others too.

Phoney Christians

What would your friends think of someone who sings sweetly in church but, once outside, says mean or nasty things? (Read verse 10 again.)

What is wrong with this picture? Put the mistakes right!

CROAK CROAK

SQUEAK SQUEAK

MOO

Don't let wrong words come from your lips!

PRAY

Dear God, may the words of my mouth be pleasing to You. Amen.

ACTION

God can help us to control our tongues if we ask Him.

Get strong!

Sort out the muddled letters to find a word which describes the little girl, the Dixons, and the people in verses 1 and 2:

d e g e r y

g _ _ _ _ y

I want another ice cream.

No! You've had enough!

Bawl
Bawl

Give me a go! It's my turn now!

Tough. I still want it ...

If you find it hard not to be like this too, you need strength to change. What five-letter word beginning with **gr_ _ _ _** describes the strength our loving God gives to us (James 4 v 6)?

PRAY

Dear Lord Jesus, give me the grace to turn away from greed, and not to love things more than You. Amen.

ACTION

If you think your temptations are too strong for you, read James 4 v 6-7 again.

A good prayer

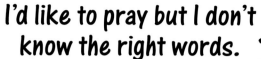

I'd like to pray but I don't know the right words.

Verse 16 tells us that God likes to hear the prayers of 'good' grown-ups and children, rather than hearing 'good' prayers.

Use this code to read the message:

⌐ = a ⌐ = b ⌐ = e
⌐ = h ⌐ = i ⌐ = l
⌐ = m ⌐ = n ⌐ = t

a	b	e
h	i	l
m	n	t

☐f you ⌐rus⌐ J⌐sus God

w☐☐☐ ⌐☐☐r your pr⌐y⌐rs.

PRAY

Dear God, thank You for knowing my feelings and thoughts even if I can't put them into words. Amen.

ACTION

God loves to hear us pray if we are trying to follow Jesus with His help.

Watch out!

Keeping to the Christian path is not always easy.

This time you don't have to follow the path in a mirror. Just see how quickly you can follow it with your pen or pencil without touching the sides. Time yourself.

TO NASTY TONGUE

TO FALSE TEACHING

TO TRUSTING MONEY

TO LIES

TO BLASPHEMY

Oh God! I'm late for the practice.

Blasphemy is wrong!

Danny is using the Lord's name as a swear word, not praying, and this is called blasphemy. But Danny might not like being told he is wrong. What should Dave do?
(Look in today's verses. Answer on page 73)

PRAY

Dear Jesus, thank You for the Bible which teaches me the true way to live with You. Amen.

BEACH BONANZA!

The Gang are off to the beach. See if you can find all the things they'll be doing or looking for whilst they're there in this wordsearch.

K	J	B	O	A	T	W	D	L	S	K	V	M	N	
M	A	E	R	C	E	C	I	O	H	B	O	Q	W	
L	O	B	W	O	F	G	K	O	E	L	A	A	V	
S	L	F	U	M	E	M	R	P	L	D	V	R	Q	
R	U	A	V	C	A	O	B	K	L	E	X	N	C	
K	W	N	B	E	K	E	Y	C	S	O	I	N	G	
E	K	O	R	T	A	E	Q	O	B	F	C	K	R	
S	Z	C	V	C	O	X	T	R	I	A	H	S	L	
I	N	B	H	I	D	O	E	D	A	P	S	E	C	
U	V	B	U	N	B	G	F	E	I	V	M	D	L	
Z	A	S	N	O	L	I	V	B	U	H	Z	N	B	
L	B	F	T	J	C	S	V	R	S	K	A	A	H	
Z	R	O	V	E	B	Y	E	I	K	Q	H	S	U	
S	U	R	F	I	N	G	F	A	A	L	N	T	O	
V	N	R	P	H	M	Y	Q	R	C	F	T	X	Z	

BEACHBALL
BOAT
BUCKET
CRABS
FISH
FOOTBALL
ICE CREAM
ROCKPOOL
SAND
SEA
SHELLS
SPADE
SUNCREAM
SURFING
WAVES

(Answer on page 73)

BALL ON THE BEACH

LAST SUNDAY ...

This Tuesday will be our Sunday School trip to the beach.

Great!

TODAY

Don't forget your lunch.

Wow – I'm pleased it's a sunny day!

I want to be prepared, it rained last year!

Paul likes to live by the Scouts' motto and be ready for anything. Here are some things the Bible tells you to be ready for: 'ready to do good' (Titus 3 v 1); 'ready for Jesus to come again' (Matthew 24 v 44).

PRAY

Father God, help me to be ready at all times to do whatever You want me to do. Amen.

BALL ON THE BEACH

God's plan is for us to enjoy life. Doing wrong things spoils life, and trusting Jesus and obeying Him brings happiness. There may be more than one way to be happy, but God's way is the best way.

PRAY

Ask God to teach you how to have a really good time with Him beside you.

BALL ON THE BEACH

Topz won't have a very nice day unless they can sort themselves out. What do you think they should do? If they all insist on having their own way they'll have no fun. Christians should to be able to sort out such problems by talking, praying and working it out together.

PRAY

If you have fallen out with a friend, ask God to show you how things can be put right.

BALL ON THE BEACH

TOPZ FOUND AN ANSWER TO THEIR PROBLEM ...

I've found a jelly fish.

Josie's caught a crab.

Help!

I've got just the place to keep all the things we find.

Topz' answer to their problem was to find something they all wanted to do together ... When you have a problem, talk to Jesus about it, and then wait quietly. Jesus will often surprise us by the way He answers our prayers and solves the problems we bring Him.

PRAY

Lord, You are really amazing. I'm glad I can turn to You to help me sort out my problems. Amen.

BALL ON THE BEACH

We'd better get back to the others.

Hey! We're surrounded.

Ouch! I've hurt my toe! I can't see the rocks.

I knew my Wellington boots would come in useful.

SPLASH!

Here, Dave, borrow my coat.

I'm sorry I laughed at you for coming in Wellingtons.

Jesus tells us not to find fault with other people. We should concentrate on getting rid of our own faults!

PRAY

Lord Jesus, please help me not to laugh at or criticise other people, but always to encourage and help them. Amen.

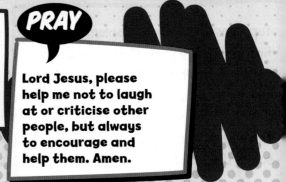

FUN AT THE BEACH

How many ball games are being played on the beach?

IT LOOKS AS IF BENNY HAS INVENTED A NEW BALL GAME OF HIS OWN!

People relax and play at the beach. Jesus lived by Lake Galilee for some years and taught the people on the beach. **Use your holidays and games to refresh your body, mind and spirit.**

PRAY

Thank You, Lord Jesus, for holidays, fun and games which make me happier and stronger in body, mind and spirit. Amen.

ACTION

When you go on holiday don't forget about Jesus!

Castles in the sand

Who won first prize in the sand castle competition? _____

Building sand castles is great fun but then the tide comes in and washes them all away.

Some people collapse or get into a state when bad things hit them. But when we trust Jesus and obey Him, He helps us through our problems.

PRAY

Lord, please help me to trust You through good times and bad times. Amen.

Our problems can be God's opportunities to help us.

Shell-shocked

How many of these shells have you seen?

Move each letter forward one place in the alphabet. a=b, b=c, z=a etc.

Some sea animals use shells as

z okzbd ne rzedsx

....

(Answer on page 73)

What do you need God to keep you safe from?

In some parts of the world shells have been used for jewellery, decorative lamps and even as money.

PRAY

Talk to God about those times when you need Him to help you feel safe.

ACTION

See if you can still remember the verse you learnt on 3rd August - Proverbs 18 v 10. 10 out of 10 if you still remembered it!

Don't be a donkey!

Look in verse 8 to find a promise God gives us, then fill in the spaces to discover what happens when we obey God.
(See verse 11)

W_ w_ll sh__t f_r j_y.

Donkeys are stubborn creatures! They like going their own way. **A lot of people are like that too!**

PRAY

Dear Lord Jesus, don't let me be like a silly donkey. Help me to listen to You, and go Your way. Amen.

ACTION

God made us, so He knows what's best for us.

Take the plunge

Shall I? Or shan't I?

Sarah's wasn't a big decision, but what should a Christian do if there is a decision or choice to make?

(Answers on page 73)

Tick the statements that agree with today's Bible verses.

1. Pray about it first.

2. Make your mind up quickly.

3. Choose whatever is easy.

4. Trust God to help you.

Have you ever had a difficult decision to make? What was it?

....

....

....

....

....

PRAY

Ask God to help with a decision you or your family have got to make.

ACTION

All our decisions are important to God: even little ones.

What if ... ?

Come on in, Paul – it's great!

What if ...

Find six words in the word square that are in verse 8.

(Answers on page 73)

T	X	O	P	N	D
Y	R	G	O	O	D
E	R	U	O	B	L
L	O	V	E	L	Y
Z	M	N	U	E	U
X	T	H	G	I	R

....
....
....
....
....
....

PRAY

Dear Lord Jesus, thank You for always looking after me. I want to love You and trust You. Amen.

God does not want you to live in fear, always thinking the worst may happen. Trust God to take good care of you.

ACTION

Try not to worry and be afraid about something which may never happen. Talk about things that frighten you, both to God and a person you can trust, and you'll find that will help.

Thanks!

Get your things together. The coach home leaves in 30 minutes.

Before we go ...

Let's thank God for all the fun we've had.

We often pray to God when we are in trouble, but how often do we pray just to say thank You because we are happy?

Write down three things you have enjoyed during the school holidays:

....

....

....

PRAY

Thank God for those things you've written down.

'... God, who generously gives us everything for our enjoyment' (1 Timothy 6 v 17).

A message from God

Dave took these snapshots at the outing. Write a title under each one.

God loves all of us just as much as He loved the people of Israel. Look at these verses again and write down something God is saying especially to you:

The people of Israel often did very silly things. Often they were not very brave or good. But look at verse 4 again: what did God think of them?

You are _ _ _ _ _ _ _ _ to me.

PRAY

Thank God for His promise to you in these verses.

ACTION

Remember, God never changes.